COLORING BOOK
PABLO PICASSO
THE MASTER OF MODERN ART

Contents

The Pipes of Pan
p. 51

Maya with Doll
p. 55

Women of Algiers
(after Delacroix)
p. 59

The Muse
p. 63

Woman Reading
p. 67

The Weeping Woman
p. 71

Portrait of Marie-Thérèse Walter
p. 75

The Kiss
p. 79

The Bathers
p. 83

*Man with Straw Hat
and Ice Cream Cone*
p. 87

Young Girl in front of a Mirror
p. 91

Colouring pencils at the ready!

Originally known as "painting books" colouring books first came into being in the 18th century, the brainchild of various painters and educationists who felt the need to promote the practice of art among young people. This enjoyable pastime, recognized as improving the cognitive ability of those who engage in it, went hand in hand with the arrival of colouring pencils, and became popular at the end of the 19th century with the appearance of the first colouring books. These were originally marketed by New York publishers McLoughlin in 1879 and became commonly used by children in the early 1930s. Colouring is an activity accessible to all, both male and female. It is a fascinating and relaxing pastime that helps to promote good motor skills and to develop concentration. Just one key quality is needed: patience. If this is something you lack at times, engaging in this very calming activity is bound to be of benefit. Whether or not you choose to follow the advice we give you here is up to you. The important thing is to let one single objective guide the way you colour: unbridled enjoyment.

Getting started

*To feel relaxed when colouring, it's a good idea to create your own space.
Gather together everything you need so that you can enjoy your colouring
without interruption.*

USING PAINTS

BRUSHES

Arm yourself with a selection of brushes of different shapes and thicknesses. Go for
quality: nothing is more annoying that a brush that loses its bristles!

PAINTS

Gouache is a very easy medium to use. Soluble and washable in water, it gives bright,
intense tones, even when heavily diluted. The colours also blend easily.

In principle, you only really need red, blue, and yellow. With these primary colours, plus a
tube of white and one of black, you can create all other colours.

It's up to you to decide how much time you want to spend mixing them!

APPLICATION

Mix your colours on a palette. Make enough to cover all the areas you'll want to paint
as it can be difficult to mix exactly the same tone again. Depending on the intensity you
want, add more or less water.

Don't overload your brush with paint, and keep a light hand. If the colour isn't intense
enough, go back over it, keeping a light touch. You'll soon find out how to adapt what
you do to obtain the desired result. And there's nothing to stop you varying thicknesses
within the same area.

USING PENCILS

COLOURING PENCILS

When choosing colouring pencils, go for "artist quality" rather than children's pencils.
Good quality pencils are softer and less dry, making it easier to blend the colours and
achieve more sustained or subtle tones. Before buying an entire set, try different pencils
out; this will help you decide which brand you prefer. Keep them in a small plastic
container within easy reach, but make sure it's stored in a safe place to prevent the pencils
from breaking.

SHARPENERS

If possible, choose a mechanical sharpener that lets you sharpen pencils of different sizes and protects the coloured lead. Failing this, go for a good quality, manual, metal sharpener which can also be useful for sharpening very short pencils. Don't press too hard when you sharpen, as you could break the lead.

ERASERS

Make sure you have vinyl erasers in different sizes so that, if necessary, you can erase very small details or small areas of colour. You can also use them to lighten colours. But be careful not to press too hard or you may damage the paper.

APPLICATION

Begin by checking that your pencils are finely sharpened: this will ensure they give the best, most even results.

You can apply colour in several layers until you obtain the colour density you want. Try one or two very light layers, then gradually increase the pressure, which should remain constant throughout the layer.

If you want to blend colours, alternate the layers. Starting with one or two common background layers, apply different colours to different areas to create a range of shades – if you want to add tone to the sky, for example.

By applying colour in small, overlapping circles, you'll avoid hard lines that can be difficult to soften. Try to work consistently, keeping the same movement and the same pressure.

DON'T FORGET

- A good, stable water pot for cleaning your brushes and diluting your paint. Change the water frequently.
- A rag to wipe your brushes or pencil leads after sharpening ... and your fingers!
- A ruler, which is useful as a guide.
- Paper tissues to absorb any surplus paint and soften pencil lines.

Pablo Picasso

Man of the world, ogre, elusive demiurge: there is no shortage of qualifiers to describe this extraordinary creator and the exceptional nature of his work. Pablo Picasso never ceased exploring new horizons, constantly reinventing himself: he was a painter, sculptor, draughtsman, engraver, and ceramicist. His vast body of work is inventive and multi-faceted, giving rise to some of the major revolutions of 20th century art. He was, without doubt, one of the most influential painters ever to defy traditional form.

The first steps of a genius

Although he lived in France, Pablo Ruiz Picasso was Spanish, Andalusian to the very core of his being. All his works are imbued with this culture. He was born on 25 October 1881 in Malaga. His father, José Ruiz Blasco, was the curator of the city museum and taught drawing at the school of fine arts. His mother, María Picasso López, whose name he also assumed in accordance with Spanish custom, was the daughter of winegrowers. In fact, he signed his early works Ruiz-Picasso and from 1901 simply Picasso. His younger sister, Dolores or Lola, was born in 1884 and the youngest, Concepción or Conchita, in 1887, though she died very young – a tragedy that affected Picasso greatly.

At a very young age, Picasso began painting at the instigation of his father who passed on to him the rudiments of this craft. He was taught the academic style. Around 1889, he painted a powdery yellow oil on wood – *The Picador* – considered to be his first painting and one he would always keep with him. He was eight years old.

In 1891, when the Malaga museum closed, the family moved to La Coruña in northwest Spain. Picasso continued painting regularly and took classes at the city's school of fine arts. In 1895, his father was appointed to teach drawing at La Lonja Academy in Barcelona. Picasso enrolled there to complete his initial training. There he met Manuel Pallarès and, in 1896, shared his first studio with him.

In 1897, at the age of 16, he passed the competitive entrance exam for the San Fernando Royal Academy in Madrid. There he explored the Prado Museum in depth and copied the work of the great masters. Becoming ill with scarlet fever, he abandoned the classes at the Academy and returned to Barcelona. He then spent a long period recuperating, including seven months at Horta de Ebro, the home village of his friend Pallarès. The following year he returned to Barcelona and produced his first compositions, which were very well received by the local academies. He also discovered the pleasures of Barcelona night life, echoes of which can be found in later works such as *The Young Ladies of Avignon*.

The blue period

In October 1900, Picasso left for Paris with his friend Carlos Casagemas, whom he had met at Els Quatre Gats café in Barcelona. He moved into a studio in Montmartre, frequenting *Le Moulin de la Galette* and the artists who performed there. He sold a few canvases to Paris art dealers. On 17 February 1901, Casagemas was driven to suicide by amorous despair, taking his life in a Paris café. Picasso, who was in Madrid at the time, was devastated. He painted a death portrait of his friend – *The Death of Casagemas* – which marked a decisive turning point in his work. From that time forward, his work was pervaded by blue. The same year, he painted the blue self-portrait that symbolizes this new stylistic inflection with dominant bluish tones and largely melancholic subjects. His figures are elongated, inspired by those of El Greco. He painted many beggars, along with patients he observed at the Saint-Lazare hospital. In September 1901, the art dealer Berthe Weill exhibited his first blue canvases alongside those of Matisse. He became friends with the painter and poet Max Jacob. In 1902, Picasso began to diversify his artistic expression, producing his first sculpture: *Seated Woman*. He then divided his time between Barcelona and Paris before settling in the Bateau-Lavoir building in Montmartre in late 1904.

The rose period and The Young Ladies of Avignon

At the end of 1904, Picasso embarked on a new period: his colour palette broadened and his themes changed. He frequented the *Circus Médrano*, close to his studio at Bateau-Lavoir. He painted circus motifs in orange and pink tones – Picasso's rose period is also known as the circus period – along with harlequin clowns and maternal female figures. He was now selling paintings more regularly and gradually leaving poverty behind. He got to know Leo and Gertrude Stein, a brother and sister who collected his work. In the autumn of 1904, he met Guillaume Apollinaire and also Fernande Olivier, with whom he fell in love. Between 1905 and 1906, his work was an uninterrupted series of formal experimentation with stylized human figures. In the spring of 1906, a meeting with Gertrude Stein led to Picasso becoming acquainted with Henri Matisse, an artist who introduced him to "negro art". Picasso also became passionate about the Iberian statuary in the Louvre. On the advice of André Derain, he visited the Trocadero ethnographic museum. It was against this background that he developed his first major work: *The Young Ladies of Avignon*. The scene is that of a brothel in Barcelona. Started in April-May 1907, Picasso completed it in July. It marks the beginning of his cubist period.

The adventure of Cubism

In the autumn of 1907, Picasso met Georges Braque through Apollinaire. For nearly 7 years, Picasso and Braque maintained a dialogue that would lead to a new artistic language: that of Cubism. This can be divided into three phases: Cezannian Cubism (1907-1909), Analytical Cubism (1909-1911) and Synthetic Cubism (1912-1914). They abandoned traditional rules (perspective, relief, local tone) and sought to process reality through simplified, geometric forms. They strove to show not one aspect of an object but several (front, side, from above) in order to produce an image as complete as possible by exploding the form into a series of interlinking planes and facets.

Picasso embarked on the geometrification of form and in 1908 began painting still-lifes. Braque and Picasso's first cubist exhibition took place at the Kahnweiler gallery. He spent the summer of 1909 in Horta de Ebro in Spain and, in September, left Bateau-Lavoir to move to Boulevard de Clichy. In 1910, Picasso and Braque took part in numerous exhibitions. In 1911, they introduced letters and numbers into their work. Picasso's relationship with Fernande ended when Éva Gouel, "Ma Jolie" in his paintings, came into his life. In September 1912, he moved to Boulevard Raspail where he produced his first collage works – *Still-life with Chair Caning* – and his first constructions, which brought the period of Analytical Cubism to an end. His father died on 3 May 1913 in Barcelona. Picasso moved to Rue Schoelcher where he produced the very fine cubist piece *Woman in a Chemise in an Armchair*, a representation of Éva Gouel. Picasso spent the summer of 1914 in Sorgues, where he produced *The Painter and his Model*, indicating the start of a new period in his work. With war declared on 2 August 1914 and Braque's departure to the Front, this period came to an end.

The Classical Period and the Ballets Russes

Picasso returned to classical compositions which reflected his admiration for the work of Ingres (this period is also known as his "Ingres period") and the influence of Greco-Roman antiquity. His melancholic figures are colossal and majestic in form, fixed in the immobility of statues.

In 1916, he received a visit from Jean Cocteau who was working with the Ballets Russes. In 1917, they joined Sergei Diaghilev and his troupe in Rome. Picasso designed the sets, costumes, and backdrop for the ballet *Parade* with music by Eric Satie. He met Igor Stravinsky and the Russian ballerina Olga Khokhlova. Between February and April he visited with Olga archaeological sites in Rome, Naples and Pompeii and the shrines of Florence. The first performance of *Parade* was given on 18 May at the Théâtre du Châtelet.

In July 1918, he married Olga Khokhlova in Paris. They lived a society life. On 4 February 1921 their first son Paulo was born. The 1920s marked the start of real recognition for Picasso that saw him offered prestigious exhibitions like that at the Art Institute of Chicago which opened in 1923.

The Surrealist Period and Guernica

One of the constants in Picasso's life was that he never allowed himself to become trapped in a movement and was always renewing the form of his art. While continuing to work on ballet sets and costumes, Picasso moved closer to the Surrealists and their leading light, André Breton, whom he met in 1923. In 1925, he took part in the "Surrealist Painting" exhibition at the Galerie Pierre. In 1927, he crossed paths with Marie-Thérèse Walter in the street; she was thirty years younger than him. She became his companion and muse. With great discretion, he moved her into an apartment on Rue de la Boëtie and, in 1930, bought the Château de Boisgeloup, near Gisors. There he set up a sculpture studio and began a series of plaster faces of Marie-Thérèse.

He worked on *The Metamorphoses*, based on the theme of the Minotaur. The figure of the Minotaur first appeared in 1928, replacing that of the Harlequin as the artist's persona. In 1932, a first major retrospective of his work was held in Paris and Zurich.

In June 1935, Picasso separated officially from Olga. Three months later, a daughter Maya was born from his union with Marie-Thérèse. In March 1936, Picasso moved in with her and their daughter in Juan-les-Pins. He was also seeing Dora Maar, a photographer he had met through Paul Éluard, whom he joined in Mougins in August. Along with Marie-Thérèse, Dora became a constant model for his female portraits during these years.

On 18 July 1936, the Spanish Civil War broke out. In January 1937, the Republican government asked Picasso to produce a large composition for the Spanish pavilion at the International Exhibition in Paris. He was left free to choose the subject. On 26 April, the town of Guernica was bombed by Hitler's air force in support of Franco. Picasso took inspiration from this and decided to create a politically engaged work denouncing the horrors of all wars. He painted this very large format work between 1 May and 7 June in his studio at 7 Rue des Grands-Augustins.

For Picasso, "painting is like keeping a diary"

From 1939 to 1945, Picasso's painting embodies the violence and desolation of the period: bodies dislocated, distorted, ripped apart using raw colours.

His mother died in Barcelona on 13 January 1939. Shortly before war was declared, Picasso took refuge at Royan, joining Marie-Thérèse and Maya who were already there. Dora Maar also joined him. He returned to Paris in August 1940. He was refused French nationality. With the Gestapo keeping a close eye on him, prohibited from exhibiting or publishing and, in 1941, threatened with extradition, he withdrew to his studio in Rue des Grands-Augustins. He was more productive than ever and wrote a piece for the theatre, *The Devil Caught by the Tail*, published by Gallimard at the Liberation. It was during these dark years that he produced the sculpture *Man with Ram*. In May 1943, he met a young artist, Françoise Gilot, who became his model, his "woman-flower". His relationships with Dora Maar and Marie-Thérèse Walter both unravelled.

More and more arrests were taking place around him and at the end of February 1944, Max Jacob was arrested and sent to the camp at Drancy where he died. On 25 August, Paris was liberated. On 5 February 1944, Picasso joined the French Communist Party. In May 1945, he completed his canvas *The Charnel House* in honour of the victims of war and his friend Robert Ruis.

Reunion with the Mediterranean

In July 1945, Picasso took his new companion Françoise Gilot to Cap-d'Antibes. Between 1946 and 1953, they spent their summers at the potters' village of Vallauris where he took over the Madoura studio and began working in ceramics. In August 1946, the curator at the Antibes Museum offered Picasso the opportunity to paint in the empty rooms of the museum, situated in the Château Grimaldi. Picasso accepted enthusiastically, producing around thirty paintings. These would remain there, along with a series of more than forty drawings, forming the core of the museum's collection. From the summer of 1948, they lived in a small house, *La Galloise*, in the hills above Vallauris, with their two children: Claude born in 1947 and Paloma born in April 1949. In February 1949, Louis Aragon chose a drawing by Picasso, *The Dove*, for the poster of the Peace Congress to be held in Paris. In the summer of 1952, Picasso met his final companion, Jacqueline Roque, in the Madoura studio. Françoise Gilot left him in 1953, taking their two children with her.

Picasso and the Masters

Up until 1962, Picasso embarked on a series of interpretations of masterpieces of art. In May 1955, he moved to *La Californie*, a villa in Cannes, with Jacqueline Roque. There he worked on variations inspired by Delacroix's *Women of Algiers*. On 11 February 1955, Olga died in Cannes at a time when the first major retrospective of Picasso's paintings was being held in Paris.

Picasso was a subject of fascination for his contemporaries, and many photographic reports and films sought to reveal the secret of his creative power, including *The Mystery of Picasso*, a documentary film by Henri-Georges Clouzot, shown at the Cannes Festival in

1956. For four months in 1957 he worked on Velázquez's *Las Meninas* (Maids of Honour), producing forty variations. In the autumn, UNESCO commissioned him to produce a wall painting for its headquarters in Paris: this was *The Fall of Icarus*. In September 1958, he bought the Château de Vauvenargues at the foot of the Sainte-Victoire mountain, beloved of Cézanne. Following his dialogue with Velázquez, in August 1959 Picasso embarked on his variations of Manet's *Luncheon on the Grass*. He moved to the farmhouse at Notre-Dame-de-Vie in Mougins. He married Jacqueline in March 1961. In November 1962, he began a series of paintings inspired by Poussin's celebrated work, *The Abduction of the Sabine Women*. This would be his final encounter with the masters who preceded him.

Picasso's final years

In November 1966, a major retrospective opened at the Grand Palais and the Petit Palais in Paris, but Picasso's health was beginning to fail. In 1967, at the height of his glory, he declined the Legion of Honour. He remained in Mougins and, between January 1969 and February 1970, produced 165 canvases with very varied subjects. In October 1971, in recognition of his 90th birthday, a selection of paintings belonging to France's public collections was exhibited in the Grand Gallery at the Louvre. The following year, Picasso painted numerous self-portraits made poignant by the presence of his dialogue with death. On 8 April 1973, Picasso died in Mougins. He was buried, according to his wishes, in the garden at the Château de Vauvenargues. Behind him he left a singular and immense oeuvre (more than 50,000 recorded works), of astonishing diversity and inventiveness that never ceases to arouse admiration.

The Dream

1932, oil on canvas
130 × 97 cm

Painted on the afternoon of 24 January 1932, this work shows Marie-Thérèse Walter, Picasso's much younger companion and lover whom he met in 1927. She quickly became one of his muses. Marie-Thérèse is shown seated, her arms resting on her stomach, her fingers interlocked, lost in peaceful sleep. Picasso skilfully translates the blend of reality and dream by integrating her facial features into the decorative motifs. Her face appears to be cut in half by the wall panelling in the background. The body also seems to melt into the décor of the room, somewhat in the manner of Matisse. Women sleeping, a recurring theme of Renaissance painting due to its erotic charge, here retains a sensual dimension. The left breast is uncovered and offered, innocently, for the pleasure of the male gaze.

The Dream, 1932

The Dream, 1932

Woman seated in front of Window

1937, oil and pastel on canvas
130 × 96 cm

Picasso painted this picture on 11 March 1937 in the studio lent to him by Ambroise Vollard at Tremblay-sur-Mauldre in Yvelines. It forms part of a long series of portraits of Marie-Thérèse Walter executed in the 1930s. The female figure is represented in interlocking geometric shapes evoking the cubist period. The colours used are less vivid than in the portraits dating from the start of their relationship. The portrait is extraordinarily classical, with Marie-Thérèse given the features of a modern-day Mona Lisa. Picasso repeats certain elements of the work by Leonardo da Vinci: the chair, the arms, and hands resting on the arms of the chair, the window in the background. The measured expression of the face recalls the enigmatic smile of its illustrious predecessor.

Woman seated in front of Window, 1937

Woman seated in front of Window, 1937

Harlequin

1901, oil on canvas
83.3 × 61.3 cm

A celebrated character of commedia dell'arte, Harlequin, a jester and clown dressed in a multi-coloured patchwork tunic, is a figure to whom Picasso often returns, a kind of imaginary extension of himself. He appears in almost all Picasso's periods (blue, rose...) and in every form (realist, Cubist...). In this painting, Picasso paints a Harlequin with a white-powdered face, his stage costume introducing a geometric touch to this naturalistic composition. The man is sitting in a café, his arm resting on a table, with an openly melancholic demeanour – probably a reference to the pain Picasso felt at the suicide of his friend Carlos Casagemas.

Harlequin, 1901

Harlequin, 1901

The Young Ladies of Avignon

1907, oil on canvas
243.9 × 233.7 cm

A masterpiece that contributed to Picasso's international renown, the subject of *The Young Ladies of Avignon* is a brothel, with its prostitutes assembled there for the pleasure of the male clients. It was painted during the winter of 1906 and completed in 1907. Picasso had thought to include two men (a sailor and a medical student) among the group of women, as can be seen from some of his preparatory drawings.

This very large format canvas turns the conventions of early 20th-century painting on their head, announcing a new era in art: that of Cubism. The composition and the way the human figures are rendered break away from realism. The influence of primitive art can also be seen in the representation of the women on the right of the painting. This mix of genres was disconcerting to the audience of the time.

The Young Ladies of Avignon, 1907

The Young Ladies of Avignon, 1907

Portrait of Dora Maar

1937, oil on canvas
92 × 65 cm

Seated on a chair in an interior defined by parallel lines that tend to geometricize the composition, Dora Maar appears to be posing for the painter. Cubism is still visible in the treatment of the facial features: the face is painted from the front and in profile. Picasso is in dialogue with the contemporary odalisques of Matisse but, while he adopts some of their features, he distances himself from them by choosing to incorporate floral motifs. The flowers that Matisse places next to his female figures here blend indistinguishably into the young woman's body: the fingers that brush against Dora Maar's face become a kind of disturbing bouquet.

Portrait of Dora Maar, 1937

Portrait of Dora Maar, 1937

Large Still Life on a Pedestal Table

1931, oil on canvas
195 × 130.5 cm

This still life is composed of a yellow jug and a bowl of fruit placed on a pedestal table. Painted on 11 March, it was one of a group of canvases Picasso produced in February and March 1931 for the exhibition at the Paul Rosenberg gallery during the summer of 1932. The composition, with its vivid colours and elegant arabesques – an explicit reference to Matisse's style of painting – met with great critical acclaim, with praise for its "cloisonnism" and the working of the colour. One can also see in Picasso's graphic choices a desire to humanize the natural representation, with fruit in the form of breasts: this work may be regarded as a cryptic portrait of the body of Marie-Thérèse Walter.

Large Still Life on a Pedestal Table, 1931

Large Still Life on a Pedestal Table, 1931

Still Life with Bull's Head

1958, oil on canvas
162.5 × 130 cm

Painted in Cannes in May and June 1958, this still life shows the imposing and disturbing skull of a bull. The skull forms part of the traditional still life repertoire. Its purpose is to recall the ephemeral nature of human life and it confers a hint of melancholy to this composition. Picasso accentuates the macabre aspect of the still life by combining the emaciated skull with its opposite: blue flowers in a vase, and the azure sky seen through the frame of the open window. The flat areas of colour applied with spontaneous, quick, and unrefined brushstrokes, like the blue spilling over the edge of the red wall, give the painting a sense of decay.

Still Life with Bull's Head, 1958

Still Life with Bull's Head, 1958

The Matador

1970, oil on canvas
114 × 145.5 cm

Between 1969 and 1971, Picasso painted a series of variations on the theme of the matador. The world of bullfighting is found throughout his works, often represented by bullfighting motifs and the bull. The theme of the matador reflects his attachment to his Spanish roots. It also demonstrates this taste for the imagery of cruelty, of sexuality, and death that pervades his work.

However, this representation of the Matador is less disturbing than those of the Minotaur that Picasso painted. This figure has a lot of the dandy and the Spanish nobleman about him: he holds his sword nonchalantly in his left hand, while smoking a cigar in his right. Picasso accentuates the sense of this character posing by painting the swirls of tobacco smoke, and the loops of his pigtail as if they were ornamental decorations.

The Matador, 1970

The Matador, 1970

The Crucifixion

1930, oil on plywood
51.6 × 66.5 cm

The theme of the crucifixion runs through Picasso's paintings, from his early works to the late 1950s. This small-scale version was painted on 7 February 1930. Despite the elongation and distortion of the human bodies, and the turbulence of the garish colours, it draws on certain elements of traditional iconography found in this episode of the Passion. Picasso depicts Golgotha as a theatrical scene in which Christ is being put to death: a small horseman thrusts his long spear into the Saviour's side in the style of Don Quixote, while some soldiers in the foreground play dice for Christ's tunic on a drum. The grimacing face at Christ's side and the long arms stretching up into the air express the emotional nature of the composition.

The Crucifixion, 1930

The Crucifixion, 1930

The Pipes of Pan

1923, oil on canvas
205 × 174 cm

This picture, painted in Antibes in the summer of 1923, is the masterpiece of Picasso's classical period. A Mediterranean atmosphere drifts through this composition showing two young men, almost naked, like shepherds from a poem by Virgil. One is playing the pipes of the god Pan, while the other appears to be listening to him with a melancholy air. Here Picasso draws on a musical theme widely developed in Venetian paintings of the Renaissance, becoming part of this cultural and aesthetic continuum. The lopsided pose of the man on the left is typical of the *contrapposto* that classical artists used to give a particular charm to their figures. The two men are placed in front of architectural features that suggest a theatre set.

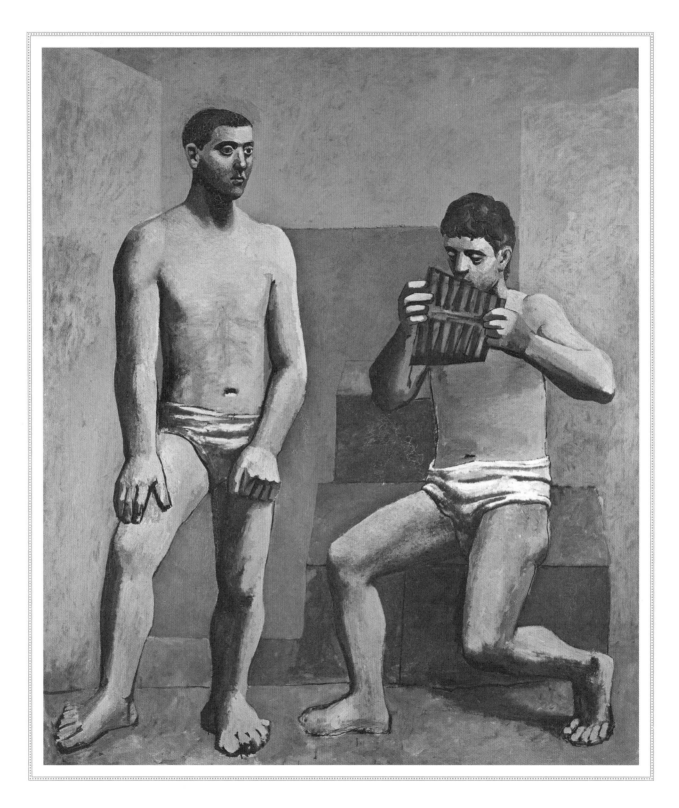

The Pipes of Pan, 1923

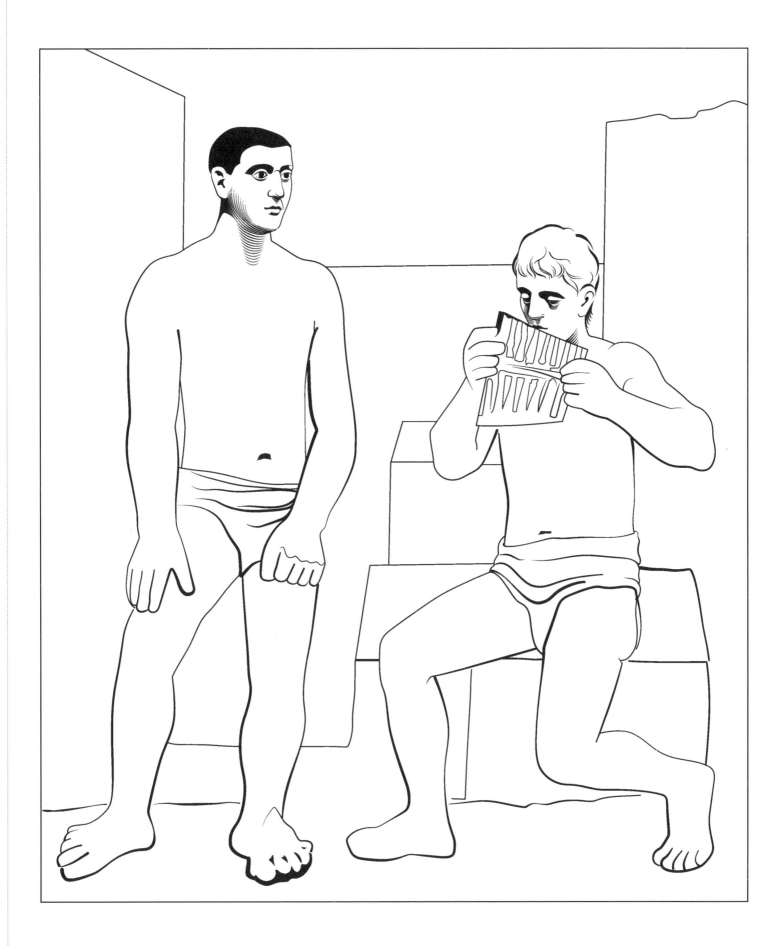

The Pipes of Pan, 1923

Maya with Doll

1938, oil on canvas

73.5 × 60 cm

This canvas, painted on 16 January 1938, shows a small, blonde, three-year-old girl with plaits. Maya was born on 5 September 1935 from the almost secret liaison between Picasso and Marie-Thérèse Walter. Her face is shown in profile and from the front, as had been Picasso's custom since Cubism.

Despite this distortion, the resemblance is maintained and the impression of life is manifest. The doll is painted as an inert object with its eyes and nose in the correct place. Maya's legs are strangely crossed and disjointed. Her right arm is painted in a childlike manner. As a child, Picasso learned to draw in the academic style; he had never "drawn like a child". With Paulo, Maya, then Claude, and Paloma, he discovered the innocence and spontaneous creativity of childhood. In Picasso there was something of a quest for lost childhood: as he said, "It has taken me my whole life to learn to paint like a child".

Maya with Doll, 1938

Maya with Doll, 1938

Women of Algiers (after Delacroix)

1955, oil on canvas
114 × 146 cm

Picasso, though the most modern of painters, was also intent on renewing the artistic codes of the past, regularly revisiting the great classic artists. Throughout his career, he returned to celebrated paintings by Poussin, Raphael, Velázquez, and, in this case, Delacroix. Picasso produced some fifteen paintings inspired by Delacroix's 1834 painting *Women of Algiers in their Apartment*. He does not copy the original work, taking only certain parts of its key elements such as the woman on the left looking at the viewer, and the door in the background. He accentuates the erotic character of the work, simply suggested by Delacroix, by placing a reclining naked woman in the foreground, and the back of another naked woman in the middle distance.

Women of Algiers (after Delacroix), 1955

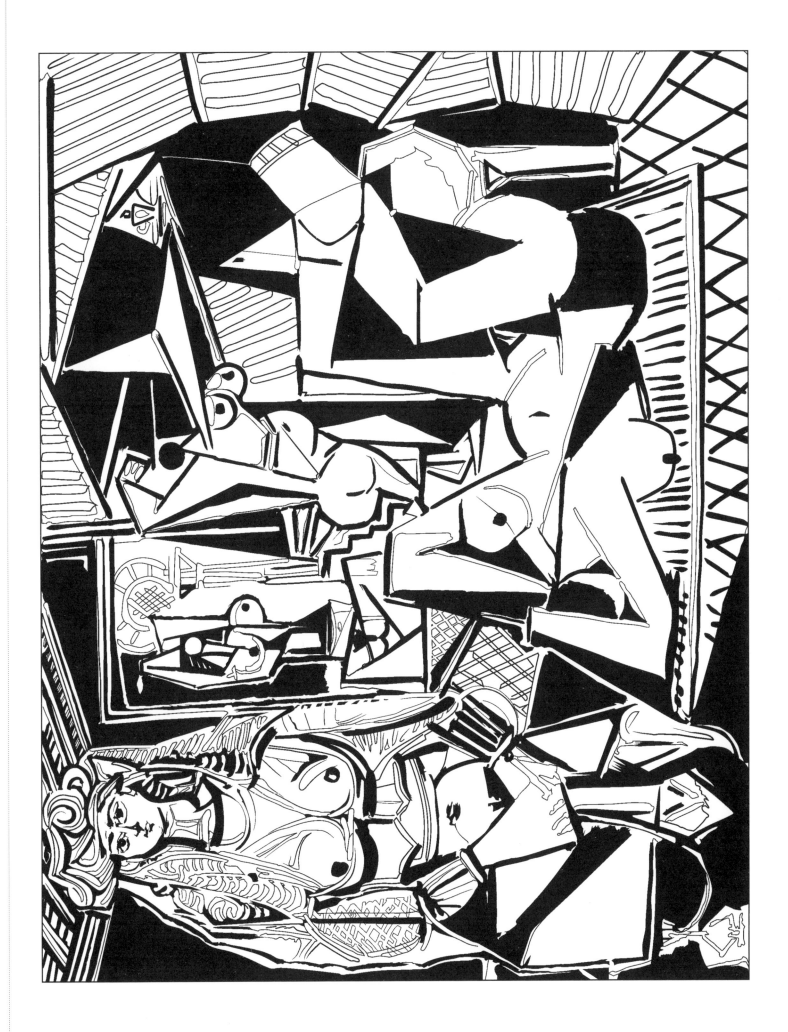

Women of Algiers (after Delacroix), 1955

The Muse

1935, oil on canvas
130 × 162 cm

Creative activity is a frequent theme in Picasso's work, both in commonplace scenes like this and through mythological or historical representations. It is through these themes that he shows the mysteries of his work. In this composition, a woman is shown drawing in front of a mirror. The association of a figure drawing, or painting, and a mirror is common in artists' self-representations. The mirror is one of the painter's customary tools and here Picasso adopts it too to signify the process of artistic creation. The reflection shows a motif that does not appear in the room where the two women are, thus transforming the mirror into a painting itself. The second woman, shown leaning on a table asleep, may be the inspirational dream figure who guides the painter's work.

The Muse, 1935

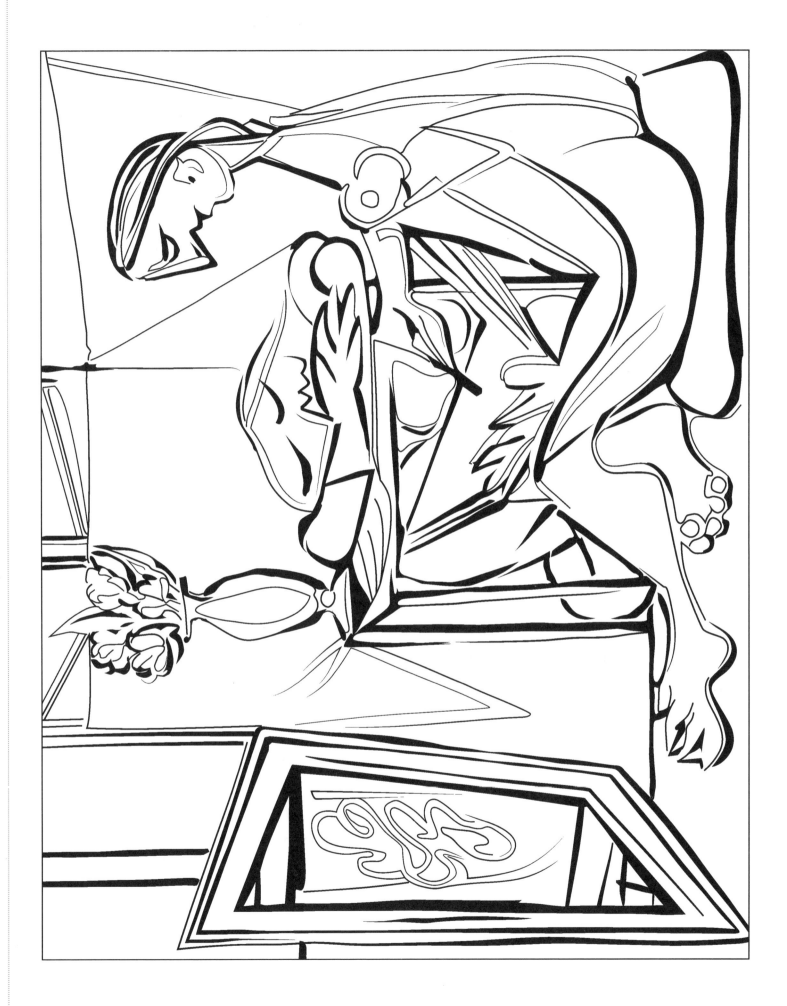

Woman Reading

1935, oil on canvas
162 × 113 cm

This work, painted on 9 January 1935, shows a young woman seated on a chair, reading a book in front of a window. The almost complete lack of depth comes from the particular use of colour and form. It accentuates the feeling of intimacy that the reading motif implies. Here, Picasso draws on a theme commonly found in 17th-century Dutch genre painting: young women writing or reading a letter in an interior. Through this implicit reference, the female figure's reading takes on an amorous connotation reinforced by the rendering of the breasts, placed at the same level as the table. The right arm, lying across the page, appears to convey a feeling of abandonment and sadness, the source of which can no doubt be found in the content of the letter she has received.

Woman Reading, 1935

Woman Reading, 1935

The Weeping Woman

1937, oil on canvas
60 × 49 cm

This canvas was painted on 26 October 1937. It depicts Picasso's lover, Dora Maar, crying. This poignant portrait may have been painted following the death of the young woman's father. Picasso captures Dora Maar in the classical pose of a "mourning woman" lamenting the loss of someone dear. He is drawing on a long tradition of devotional art, showing the Virgin Mary distraught at the death of her Son. She holds a handkerchief that she appears to be biting, thus heightening the emotional charge of the image which the Cubist orientation, still visible in this picture through the human figure cut into geometric blocks, serves to accentuate. Picasso often shows Dora Maar in a dramatic manner, with tortured form, revealing his lover's true, melancholic, and troubled nature.

The Weeping Woman, 1937

The Weeping Woman, 1937

Portrait of
Marie-Thérèse Walter

1937, oil on canvas
100 × 81 cm

The similarity between the *Portrait of Dora Maar*, also painted in 1937, and that of Marie-Thérèse Walter is not, of course, unintentional on Picasso's part: as his amorous conquests grow, he engages, through this visual rapprochement, in a strange duplicitous game which places the two women in competition. The pose is borrowed from Ingres' work *Madame Moitessier Seated*, painted in 1856. The portrait of Marie-Thérèse Walter adopts the same attitude ,with her hand delicately placed against her cheek. Once again, Picasso draws on pictorial tradition with this clear allusion to Ingres, the embodiment of the classical ideal of French painting. However, he alters the original model through the distortion of the body, giving this portrait a less evanescent air than that of Ingres.

Portrait of Marie-Thérèse Walter, 1937

Portrait of Marie-Thérèse Walter, 1937

The Kiss

1925, oil on canvas
130.5 × 97.7 cm

As so often with Picasso, the more or less geometric graphic forms, which seem to suggest a simple, abstract composition are used here to evoke human bodies. In this canvas, painted during the summer of 1925 in Juan-les-Pins, one can discover, behind the informal aspect of the scene, a man and woman intertwined. Eyes, a mouth, a beard, and arms appear from this interlacing of the forms, suggesting a passionate kiss. The lovers' bodies are intimately melded, making it impossible to distinguish one from the other. This confusion of identities and the distortion of the architecture of the human body are a visual transcription of the amorous passion of this kiss incarnate.

The Kiss, 1925

The Kiss, 1925

The Bathers

1918, oil on canvas

27 × 22 cm

Produced in Biarritz in the summer of 1918, at the end of the First World War, this small format canvas evokes the rediscovery of simple pleasures. For Picasso, the carefree nature of life on the coast was a frequent motif in paintings of children and adults playing on the beach. Here the bathers, treated in an almost classical style, are not naked as in ancient art or as in certain works by Courbet and Cézanne. They are wearing fashionable bathing suits and drying their hair in the breeze; in the background is the jetty and lighthouse at Pointe Saint Martin in Biarritz. Through her dynamic stance, the bather standing in a blue and white striped costume evokes the Maenads of Greek mythology: is she brushing her hair, or tearing it out in lamentation?

The Bathers, 1918

The Bathers, 1918

Man with Straw Hat and Ice Cream Cone

1938, oil on canvas
61 × 46 cm

This painting is one of the innumerable portraits Picasso produced throughout his life. Picasso freely varied his treatment of the traditional portrait genre, ranging from realism to Cubism in his depiction of the human face. This portrait, painted in August 1938, shows a man eating an ice cream and sporting a straw hat, perhaps in homage to Van Gogh and his *Self Portrait with Straw Hat*. Picasso plays with physical distortion, giving this piece a playful character. The motif is anecdotal; it does not draw on the great themes of historic portraiture. Picasso often uses the iconography of the everyday which contrasts sharply with the exuberance of the pictorial treatment. The man's tongue, emerging from his mouth like a snake, and the enormous fingers clumsily holding the cornet contribute to the strangeness of the composition.

Man with Straw Hat and Ice Cream Cone, 1938

Man with Straw Hat and Ice Cream Cone, 1938

Young Girl in front of a Mirror

1932, oil on canvas
162.3 × 130.2 cm

Picasso treats this intimate and apparently commonplace scene of a woman looking at herself in a mirror in an extremely refined way. By giving his young lover, Marie-Thérèse Walter, the classical posture of Venus with a mirror, Picasso magnifies the erotic aspect of the young woman, a source of desire and inexhaustible inspiration for the artist. This confrontation of Marie-Thérèse with her image also possesses a moral value imbued on it by Vanitas art. The change of appearance in the woman's reflection, with its transformation of colour and the tight framing of the rounded belly, evokes a "reflection" on passing time and the metamorphosis of a child into a woman. The representation of Marie-Thérèse's face from the front and in profile suggests this duality in another way.

Young Girl in front of a Mirror, 1932

Young Girl in front of a Mirror, 1932